SCOTLAND
HEBRIDES BY MOTORBIKE
Stephen and Scharlie Platt

www.leveretpublishing.com

Scotland: Hebrides by Motorbike
First published - November 2024
Published by Leveret Publishing
56 Covent Garden, Cambridge, CB1 2HR, UK

Lewis chessmen Warder-Berserker

ISBN 978-1-912460-74-8

© Stephen Platt 2024

All rights reserved. No part of this publication may be reproduced, stored in a retrieval system or transmitted in any form by any means, electronic, mechanical, photocopying, recording or otherwise, except brief extracts for the purpose of review, without the written permission of the publisher.

HEBRIDES 2016

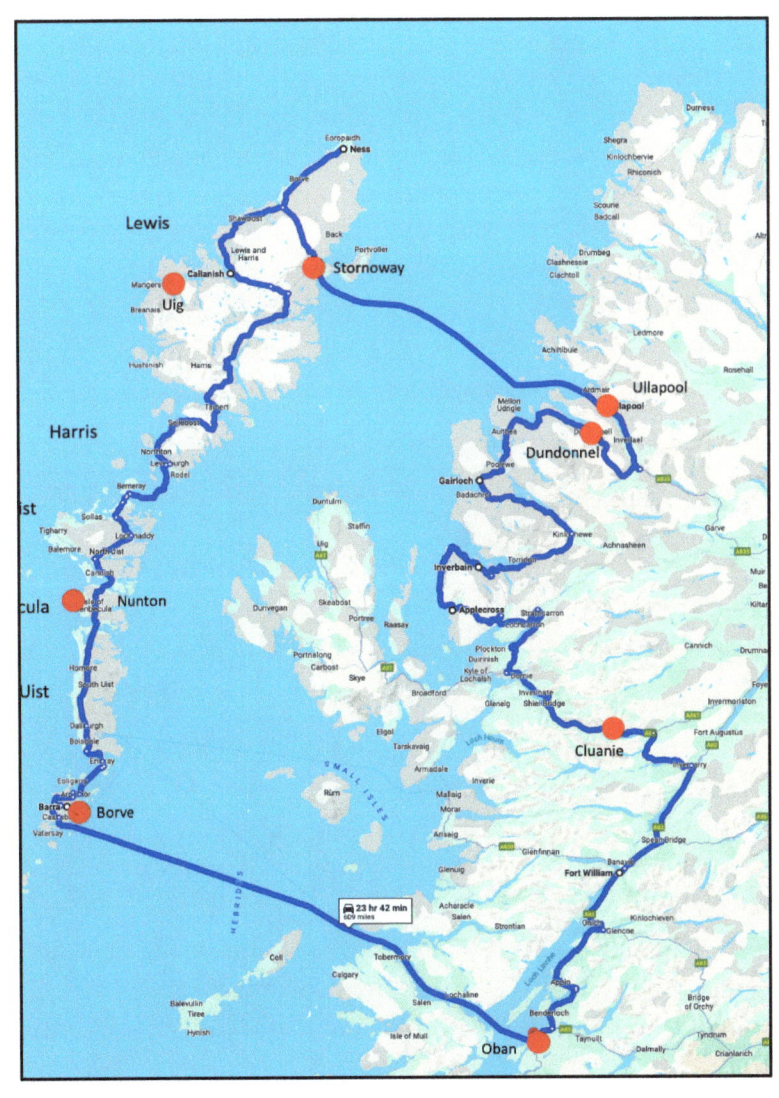

Day 1 Home to Milngavie 257 miles

Tuesday 21 June 2016

I felt I was getting too old for the bike, a BMW 100RS first registered in 1988. For those who don't know bikes, it was like the big white bikes motorcycle police used to use. It had a top speed of 120 mph and we had done 115mph on it hurrying back from the Alps. I bought it in 1994 and we had toured with it in France, Italy, Ireland and Scotland. It was a most comfortable bike whether hammering across France on motorways or pottering along country roads in Ireland, low revving like a sewing machine. But it was heavy, especially when laden with our camping and climbing gear. And we'd had enough of riding long stretches of motorway.

We hadn't ridden it for a while and I was tempted to sell it and perhaps get a lighter bike. But I wanted to see if we could have one last big road trip and had always fancied the Outer Hebrides. Five years earlier I had bought a Motolug trailer so we could tow the bike behind the car. The

The bike – BMW R100RS 998cc 1988

nice thing was it was collapsible and could be stowed in the boot of the car. The plan was to drive to Oban, towing the bike, and leave the car and trailer there while we toured the Hebrides and the West Coast of Scotland on the bike.

The bike had two side cases or panniers, which as well as clothes, contained our lightweight tent and sleeping bags. I also had a large tank bag that packed all my kit. Our waffle sleeping mats were strapped to the rear pannier and gave Scharlie some back support. The cooking pan and stove slipped into the space between the fairing and forks.

Getting the bike onto the trailer was tricky. First I had to remember how to assemble the parts. This involved opening the two hinged parts of the frame to trap the axle. Then the wheels were threaded onto either end of the axle and the trailer hitched to the car's ball hitch tow with its lighting relay.

The clever thing about the trailer was that the angle at which it tilted to the car could be varied by means of a swivel joint just behind the ball hitch. This allowed the rear of the trailer to touch the ground and form a ramp so the bike could be pushed up into place and then the tilt adjusted

The trailer – Motolug

to level the bike for transportation. This seemed simple as I rehearsed the moves in my mind. But, as I said earlier, the bike was getting too heavy for me and I was nervous about driving it up the ramp. Nevertheless I managed it alright, controlling the power with the throttle and clutch and walking to the side of the bike as it rode up the trailer, being careful not to let it run away with me. Then I used the ratchet straps to fasten it down, two on the front forks and two either side of the pannier frame to the rear.

We set off and drove to Glasgow, but on a roundabout near Malcolm's house in Milngavie, where we were going to spend the night, one of the straps holding the bike to the trailer came loose and the bike tipped over. Luckily the restraining cup holding the front wheel stopped it falling over. But what we didn't realise was that the strain on the wheel and tire was to cause us problems later.

Malcolm and Doreen's house in Milngavie

Day 2 The Cobbler and Inverary 55 miles

Wednesday 22 June 2016

We followed Malcom's car out of Milngavie and headed north. We planned to do a walk and a scramble on the way and Malcolm would need his car to get back home. It's a pretty drive along the west side of Loch Lomond with views across the loch to Ben Lomond. Turn left at Tarbett and find somewhere to park0 at the village of Succoth, at the head of Loch Long.

The Cobbler, also known as Ben Arthur, is at the head of Loch Lomond and has some of the best rock climbing in the Southern Highlands. It is regarded as a hard and challenging route. It involves a seven mile (11 km) walk in along easy paths ascending 920m. But that's not the hard bit. It's the last few metres that involve some serious scrambling and intimidating exposed moves that create the challenge. It is named for its large rocky summit features which are supposed to represent a cobbler bending over

The Cobbler

Boulangerie and cafe

Scharlie on the ramp

his last.

A newly constructed path by-passes the tramway that the original route followed and zigzags up the hillside through an area of forestry. This path meets up with the old tramway path and continues from there, following the Allt a' Bhalachain. From here the path bypasses the Narnain Boulders, steepening at around 600 metres (2,000 ft). Nearer the top, it flattens out at a bealach, which is marked by a cairn.

The Cobbler has three distinct peaks. The high point of the central peak can only be reached by a grade 3 exposed scramble. The ancient early Cambrian rock is a metamorphosed sedimentary schist and is sound and offers good holds.

Standing below the summit block it looks precarious and unstable and devoid of an easy ascent. But a rocky ramp leads round the right hand side of the pinnacle to a hole that passes through the body of the tower below the summit. Having negotiated the ramp, the next step is to thread the eye of the needle and crawl through this hole. On the other side of the hole is an intimidating ledge that slopes upwards to the summit. At the far end of the ledge a scramble of good holds leads to the summit blocks.

The summit blocks

Threading the needle

Deep cracks fissure the rock and the summit appears like an untidy pile of children's blocks. All three of us managed the ascent and crowded together on the summit and took photos. The summit commands fine views and many hills can be seen including the nearby Bein Ime and Bein Narnain and the more distant Ben Cruachan, Ben More and Ben Vorlich. The way down involves reversing the route, much harder of course but again we all managed without any drama.

Malcolm went back to Milngavie and we drive to Inverary where we will spend the night at the Brambles. The A83 is another beautiful stretch of road, by Loch Long, then over the hills by the Old Military Road, by the side of the Kinglas Water and finally following the north side of Loch Fyne.

Inveraray is small attractive town in Argyll and Bute on the shore of Loch Fyne and is the ancestral seat of the Dukes of Argyll, chiefs of the Clan Campbell. The current Inverary Castle is a grand Georgian mansion designed by architects William Adam and Roger Morris in the mid 18h Century. The four-star Brambles Hotel and restaurant, where we're staying, is on the main street. There is no hotel parking so we parked on the road and left the bike on the trailer.

Loch Long and Arrochar

Brambles of Inverary

Day 3 Inverary to Barra via Oban 40 miles

Thursday 23 June 2016

Yesterday Great Britain voted to leave the EU 51.9% to 48.1%. Scharlie had a terrible night in Inveraray in spite of being in a very plush suite with two enormous double beds. She said it was because she was anxious about the referendum while still daring to hope that we would wake to good news. Now her spirits are low in spite of where we are – fulfilling a dream of going to the Outer Hebrides. Cameron has said he will resign as PM and a new leader will be elected in October. "It's the democratic will of the people of Britain and will be respected", he says. What a cock-up. The young want to remain while the old want to leave. What does that say about the future?

It is less than 40 miles to Oban and takes about an hour. The A819 is a single land rural road bordered by mixed woodland and green fields. So we arrived in good time. We rode along the front through the holiday

Oban

CalMac ferry

Kismul cafe Castlebay

traffic and found the garage parking where we planned to leave the car. It was hard work getting the bike off the trailer, the trailer disassembled and fitted into the car and repacking all the stuff we needed to take with us. Finally we were ready. We shunted the car into a tight corner in the yard and climbed on the motorbike and set off for the port.

It's a calm bright day and the ferry rocks gently across the furrowed ocean, cleaving a way through dancing specs of light. The curved horizon a dusky pink line dividing deep blue sea from paler sky. The CalMac ferry takes five hours. The first stretch runs between Mull and the mainland and then crosses the Sea of the Hebrides, a Marine Protected Area with basking shark and minke whales.

From the ferry we rode up the Pier Road towards the church on the hill above the village. Our Lady, Star of the Sea is a Catholic Church. The Protestant Reformation never made an impact on Barra and largely due to the success of the Irish missionaries Barra has remained predominately Roman Catholic.

Kismul Castle

We have fish and chips, fresh and crisp, at the Cafe Kisimul, a family run curry cafe near the harbour. We sit outside on the wooden picnic benches and have a wonderful view of Kisimul Castle built on a rocky inlet out in the bay only 200 metres from the shore. We talk to a man about travelling on his own and sleeping in his van. He is wildlife painter living near Edinburgh but comes to these islands frequently. He recommended going to a Gaelic church on Sunday to hear the singing.

There's a marathon in Barra so we are camping tonight as everywhere is booked. We learn that there is a campsite three or four miles up the west coast at Borve. We just squeaked into the camp site and pitched our tiny tent before the owner turned up on the grass verge at the edge of the sands. He let us stay as we were only there for one night. We are right next to the sea but don't see the dolphins that sometimes come in. The washing and cooking facilities are spotless and it's a great site with marvellous views.

Campsite at Borve

Day 4 Barra to Benbecula via South Uist 45 miles

Friday 24 June 2016

We slept well, in spite of the previous restless night and being squashed into a small tent. The weather overnight was fine but it's not so good this morning. We drive around Barra to catch the small ferry from Ardmòr to Eriskay. The painter was there in his van; he's staying with a Belgian friend in North Uist. Like us he is dismayed by the referendum result. His friend has lived here for years but isn't a British citizen. The ferry took only forty minutes and it was grey and rainy as we landed and we stopped in a cafe for breakfast. Two cyclists who we had seen on the ferry joined us. From Eriskay there is a straight stone causeway to South Uist.

We had a smooth ride along the flat west coast of South Uist. It was drizzling and Beinn Mhor and Heacla were shrouded in mist. The big fairing kept us dry, but it was disappointing that the weather was so poor. We stopped to take photos of a beached fishing boat in the style of Viking

Borve beach

long boat. The cream-white rendered houses and bungalows seem scattered randomly over the landscape. On a bright sunny day they would have looked pleasing but in the mist shrouded rain the landscape seemed somewhat forlorn.

The Highland clearances had a devastating effect on this part of Scotland. Families were evicted from farms in the glens to crofts on the coast and then, when they kelp industry collapsed and the potato famine hit, clan chiefs and land owners paid their passage to America and Australia. Only in recent years has the population begun to recover as communities have taken control and tourism has provided an income. But the pattern of small holdings and scattered settlement along the coast persists.

We pressed on along the single track Rubha Ban, going slowly and taking care on the wet road. We crossed over to Benbecula via a short causeway where the road hugs the west coast to avoid an area of hundreds of small lakes. We found a great bunkhouse for the night at Baile nan Cailleach, a tiny hamlet with a chapel and burial ground that go back to the time of St Columba in the 6th Century. Nunton House is run by Donald and is part of an independent Scottish chain of bunk houses. There was only one

Borve standing stane

other guest – a government development inspector of some sort, so we had a room and an ensuite bathroom to ourselves. The hostel has a great sitting room with inglenook fireplace and good cooking facilities with milk cereal and bread provided. It was most comfy and friendly.

The inspector said all the new infrastructure and improvement of ferry ports was EU funded. He thought England was in for a hard time and Nicola Sturgeon was already lining up Scotland to leave the Union. Maybe all is not lost, said Scharlie, Cameron hasn't informed the EU yet. Maybe the people will succeed in asking for a referendum rerun. We have to accept the vote or the democratic system will be brought into disrepute, said the inspector. Scharlie said she still felt that some legal way could be found if a strong leader who cared about the country rather than his or her party was to emerge to represent the groundswell of thinking public opinion. Apart from the petition to rerun the referendum that Steve has signed on his phone we are very short of news. We hear there is a vote of no-confidence in Jeremy Corbyn today but no news of other initiatives. Boris claims we have a brilliant opportunity in front of us!

Nunton House, Benbecula

Day 5 Benbecula to Lewis   113 miles

Sunday 25 June 2016

The weather is really wet and the ride over the short causeway and across North Uist is depressing. We decide to catch the 10.30 ferry to Harris. It would be lovely to stay and explore Uist more but this is a reconnaissance trip we tell ourselves, although we know in our hearts it is unlikely we will return. It's such a pity because the hills and the beaches look so beautiful in the photographs we've seen. We have a wet, unpleasant ride to the ferry but we know the route as we had an evening ride round the coast last night in the late evening sunshine. There is another short causeway across to the tiny island of Berneray to reach the little ferry terminal and a small unheated shed with loos and a waiting room but we find to our dismay that the 10.30 ferry doesn't run on Sundays. The book noticeboard was flashing the next one for 4:30 PM but the timetable said 1 PM.

The cycling duo had made the same mistake as us but they seemed

Benbecula causeway

unfazed and settled down to play Scrabble. Scharlie was seized with extreme restless impatience and was striding about to keep warm. The time went slowly and she couldn't even write her diary as she couldn't find her pen. So she paced disgruntled, but admiring of the cyclists sang froid.

About 12 PM the ferry arrived and let off the cars. Steve checked and confirmed that it would leave at 1 PM but it disappeared to refuel. Gradually the waiting room filled with more wet cyclists arriving in damp shorts and bare legs. Scharlie's teeth were chattering so she was amazed that they seemed quite relaxed.

The ferry returned and left promptly at 1PM. Only a short run, but it was an opportunity to warm up before setting off again in the rain. The ferry threads its way between tiny islands to reach Leverburgh on Harris. We were so disappointed having been looking forward to savouring the beauties of Harris. The Cyclists following the "Golden Road" up the islands said they had had great weather so far and look suntanned. We had booked into another bunkhouse in the north of Lewis on the advice of Donald, so had a long way to go. A showery hour's ride brought us to a pub in Tarbert, the Hotel Hebrides, possibly the only place open on

Ferry North Uist to Harris

Sunday. It was delightfully warm and we ordered fishcakes and enjoyed a respite from the rain for an hour.

Scharlie had a signal and texted Helen. We had just set off again when Helen rang to say she thought we'd like to know that Phoebe has just returned from her Duke of Edinburgh weekend. She suffered muddy cold and hunger as her group had mislaid their food! She was headed straight for the shower. It was lovely to hear Helen's voice but we couldn't talk long as the drizzle intensified and we had another two hours in front of us.

A long windy cold two hours coming across Harris with nothing to do but grit our teeth and endure the cold air and drizzle insinuating itself down our necks and up our sleeves. Scharlie's views from her seat on the pillion were unremittingly grey and she had no sense of time or how long it would be.

We had a bad moment when we stopped for a break on the uneven road verge. Before we knew it we were sprawled on the road beside a horizontal bike with the petrol spewing out. After turning off the petrol, we tried to lift the heavy bike laden with camping gear and luggage, but to no avail. Then round the corner came a little Morris Minor car with two

Fishing boat in the spirit of the Vikings

elderly but sprightly ladies who jumped out, their tweed skirts flapping in the wind. They offered to help. Steve was skeptical, but working together the four of us got the bike upright and stable. They were sisters and seemed to know something about bikes and admired our machine. You're a brave lady they said and made sure we were quite all right before leaving us.

We had planned to try and attend a church to listen to the singing which we'd heard was famous, but we were too late for the morning service at the North Harris Free Church in Tarbett. At Aird Asaig we had a brief view of a white sandy bay curving below us before heading off into the foggy mountains of Harris. The road wasn't too steep and the bends weren't too sharp, but the rain was sleeting down and it felt serious.

The bunkhouse at Uig Bay was lovely and run by another Donald who had built it a year ago on his own land on the loch shore. To get there we followed the main road nearly into Stornoway before turning northwest and then along a minor road round to Gallan Head.

We had parked the bike on the roadside above the cabin as Steve didn't want to run the risk of dropping it on the steep gravel hill down to

Ottewr bunkhouse

Otter bunkhouse

Tràigh na Beirigh sands

the bunkhouse. A neighbour came out to approve our parking place. He and the two ladies with him were dressed very smartly in Sunday best with hats and sped off in a car to the Kirk for evensong. We were too cold and wet to follow them and needed to rest.

The Otter Bunkhouse is small and very cosy and the living room sofa gave an uninterrupted view of the water and the mountains on the other side. Scharlie was so chilled that she wrapped herself in a blanket and moved very little for the rest of the evening.

Donald came in to collect his money and told us that otters were often seen just below the bunkhouse but usually at high tide, which came in the middle of the night so we would most likely miss them. He was a friendly man who seemed more interested in providing employment for young people in the area than making money from his bunkhouse. We asked him if he got many visitors – we were the only ones that night. Enough to keep the house alive, he said.

When we were getting ready to leave the next morning the gentleman we'd seen in his Sunday best, dressed now in oilskins, waved us goodbye.

Timsgarry

Tràigh Uige sands

Tràigh Uige sands and dunes

Day 6 Lewis and Stornoway 81 miles

Sunday 26 July 2016

Next morning was bright and clear so we decided to explore the local area around Uig. We went to a beach where 93 Viking chess pieces were found buried in the dunes in a small stone kist or chamber on the edge of the beach by a Malcom MacLeod in 1831. They were carved from walrus ivory and thought to have been made in Norway, possibly in Trondheim, in the 12th Century during years that the Norse ruled Scotland. Eleven of them are in National Museum in Edinburgh and 82 are in the British Museum in London.

There is a large replica wooden carving of a chess piece King carved by Stephen Hayward that marks the spot. The white sand beach curled round the whole bay, fringed with seagrass waving in the fierce breeze. We found a sheltered place out of the wind beside a small cliff to enjoy the sunshine.

Tràigh Uige sands

Tràigh Uige sands

Lewis Chessman – King

We rode down to Ardroil beach at Uig Sands and went exploring the beach and dunes. The rock is pink granite and the sand pale creamy yellow. It must be one of the most beautiful beaches in Scotland. It was sunny but chilly in the breeze and we had to keep muffled up in our winter clothes. Leaving the beach on a grass track we had a close call with an oncoming vehicle that left us very little room to pass. Steve's nerve was impressive as we squeaked round.

Our next stop was the standing stones at Callanish – amazingly like Stonehenge but as yet unfenced and quite open to the public. The stones are a cruciform with a central stone circle of thirteen stones with a monolith near the middle. They were erected in the late Neolithic and were a focus for ritual activity during the Bronze Age. The stones are all of the same rock, the local Lewisian gneiss. The stone circle was set up between 2900 and 2600 BC and abandoned about 800 BC. According to one tradition, the Callanish Stones were petrified giants who would not convert to Christianity.

The central monolith is 4.8 metres high and the largest sides are almost perfectly oriented to the north and south. We wandered around the

Callanish standing stones

Callanish monolith

stones for a while before another wet front came through and we ran to the tearooms for shelter where we bought a Harris tweed hat and brooch for Jessica. Looking at the map later we realised that they weren't the only standing stones in the area, there were half a dozen other stone circles within a mile radius.

Then on to the Broch at Dun Carloway, an impressive, fortified dwelling of stone like a huge beehive. The broch is on a rocky knoll in a good defensive position. It was built in the Iron Age to impress and defend and was probably the home of a tribal leader. It is constructed as two concentric walls of stone, with a stairway or gallery within the walls to the upper floors. The Carloway Broch is one of the best preserved in the Hebrides and dates back over 2000 years. It is approximately 9 metres high and 15 metres in diameter.

Callanish Visitor Centre

Spiral staircase between inner and out wall

Entrance to stairway

The story goes that the Morrisons of Ness had stolen cattle from the MacAuleys of Uig. The MacAuleys wanted their cattle back and found the Morrisons in the broch. Donald Cam MacAuley climbed the outer wall using two daggers and smoked out the Morrisons by throwing burning heather into the broch. The MacAuleys then destroyed the broch.

By the middle of the 19th century a large portion of the top of the wall had disappeared, the stones being re-used in other buildings. But one side of the broch still rises to nearly 9 metres and is most impressive. We clambered about it, climbing the spiral stairway and popping out through holes in the inner wall.

The weather was still uncertain so after this we headed for our hotel in Stornoway.

The Carloway Broch

Cuanna House, Stornoway

Day 7 Stornoway to Little Loch Broom 26 miles

Monday 27 July 2016

Perhaps because we knew it would be demanding riding the motorbike in all weathers or perhaps because this was our last big bike ride I had booked nice hotels for the rest of the trip. Last night we slept in Cuanna House, a small B&B close to the ferry terminal, handy since we would be catching an early morning ferry. It was all it promised – warm, comfortable, an excellent breakfast and free parking right in front.

It was only a three or four minute ride to the ferry terminal and we were in good time. Strapping the bike to the steel wall of the car deck with the help of one of the crew I noticed that the front tire was flat and realised that the near spill we had had in Glasgow at the start of the trip had finally caught up with us and the tubeless tire was no longer making an air-tight seal on the wheel rim.

Ferry from Stornoway to Ullapool

We stayed on deck looking towards the Achiltibue and the Summer Isles on the CalMac ferry (Caledonian MacBrayne) from Stornoway to Ullapool.

I Googled garages and found Loch Broom Garage Services in Ullapool. They were fantastic, taking off the wheel and taking pains to get a good seal, which wasn't easy. Now we could begin the road trip we had been looking forward to with confidence. We planned to hug the West coast as far as Oban, taking minor roads. The weather had improved and our spirits lifted.

Our next stop was Dundonnel House at the head of Little Loch Broom. It is only 25 miles from Ullapool following Loch Broom inland and then swinging back north to reach Dundonnel. I had been here before when I climbed An Teallach in September 2012 and had tea in the hotel before driving back to Scharlie's parents house in Coniston. An Teallach (1062m) is perhaps the hardest Munro I climbed. If you follow the ridge and climb all the rock towers it is challenging since some of the scrambles are intimidating on your own. The lounge was crowded when we arrived, but we managed to find two comfy easy chairs and order tea and cake. Our room had a view of the loch.

Loch Broom Garage, Ullapool

An Teallach pinnacles

An Teallach (1062m)

Day 8 Little Loch Broom to Loch Cluanie   174 miles

Tuesday 28 July 2016

Today is the big day when we ride the coast road round Wester Ross. After a hearty breakfast we set forth along the A832 following Little Loch Broom to Badcaul. It's clear and sunny with high wispy cirrus clouds and the weather looks set fair at last. The gorse by the side of the road is bright yellow, the sky is blue, the heather purple, and for once the mountains look inviting rather than forbidding. We pulled into a layby to view the calm waters of the loch.

The road climbs to moorland with occasional fir plantations then drops down to the sea at Mungasdale. It's most pleasant riding the motorbike on a quiet road in fine weather. The views are marvellous and we are just pottering along fairly sedately and the bike is purring contentedly. We pass Gruinard Island just off the coast and white sand beaches and enchanting rivers with views of the heather hills and the blue sea.

Little Loch Broom A832

Gruinard Island

Drium Breac, Rubha Mòr peninsula

We head inland to cross the Rubha Mòr peninsula to Drumchork. Now we are riding along the shores of Loch Ewe with splendid views across to the Isle of Ewe. There is a pier at Aultbea and a jetty on the island and a few scattered homesteads. It is in habited by a single extended family, the Grants, that rely on supplies coming over by boat. The island previously had more families, but they left during the Second World War, when Loch Ewe was used as a naval anchorage. Its position meant that the children had to endure a round trip each day of about 26 miles by boat and bus to attend school. The island remains off grid and the only physical connection to the mainland is a single phone line.

Our next stop was at Inverewe Garden, widely regarded as one of the most beautiful gardens in Scotland. Here, thanks to the warming Gulf Stream, a father and daughter had created a wonderful loch side garden amid the rugged moorland. This lush, almost tropical seeming oasis was created out of bare rock and a few scrub willows in 1862 by Osgood Mackenzie and is full of colourful, exotic plants from around the world. Highlights include the most northerly planting of rare Wollemi pines, Himalayan blue poppies, olearia from New Zealand, Tasmanian eucalypts,

Drumchork

Loch Ewe

Inverewe gardens

and rhododendrons from China, Nepal and the Indian subcontinent. We spend an hour or so wandering around the terraces admiring the sculptures and pools and noting some of the plants and trees.

This is the perfect motorbike road. The surface of the road is excellent and the constant gentle bends delightful rather than exciting or challenging. We are now getting distant views of the mountains of Torridon. And looking east we could see the mountains of Fisherfield Forest and Letterewe Forest south of Fionn Loch. I was there in 1969, walking the eleven miles from Poolewe to remote and fantastic Carnmore Crag with Malcolm and friends from the Manchester University Mountaineering Club. We stayed in the Carnmore bothy for a week and, among other things, climbed Dragon, Fionn Buttress and Gob.

Poolewe was a mini metropolis compared with the isolated country we'd been through. Then over the moors with views of Loch Maree to the southeast and on to Gairloch where we stopped for a break at the farm shop. There is more development now by the side of Gairloch. This is the land of the clan Mackenzie and a thousand years ago the loch was a haven for Viking long boats. Gairloch beach to the south of the village is quite

Inverewe Garden

unspoilt. We ride through woodland and then by the side of the River Kerry past Loch Bad an Sgalaig and then along Loch Maree with a great view of Slioch (980m).

At Kinlochewe we turn right along the single carriageway A896. The road was good and there were plenty of passing places. The hills of Glen Torridon are wilder than the moors we came through earlier. We are below the mighty Beinn Eighe (993m) and at various points of the road have views of the summit ridge.

At Loch Bharranch we get a splendid view of Liathach (1055m) one of the finest Scottish mountains and, of the places we'd been, only rivalled by Ladhar Bheinn in Noydart and the Cuillin Ridge. I was here in June 2012 on one of my solo one night dashes from the Lakes. I drove up the night before and slept in the car in a layby below Liathach. There was a path at first by the side of a stream descending from Stuc a Choire Dhuibh Bhig the eastern most summit of the Liathach ridge. Moving west along the rocky pinnacles involves a hands on exposed traverse of Am Fasarinen. At Mullach an Rathain at the western end of the ridge you drop down by the side of waterfalls and a four mile walk along the road back to the car.

Liathach Torridon

Beinn Alligin, Torridon

Loch Shieldaig

Scharlie and I had climbed Beinn Alligin, with its equally exciting ridge, the Horns of Alligin, in April 2010.

We don't linger in Torridon despite our fond memories of staying here, but head for Shieldaig. We are back on a two lane carriageway and stop at a viewpoint on Upper Loch Torridon where there is a great view across to Beinn Alligin. There are picnic benches in front of the Shieldaig Bar and we stop for a welcome rest and admire the view of the Loch and Shieldaig island.

The road soon becomes a single carriageway again but instead of continuing along the A896 we turn off along the coast road to Applecross. The road is narrow, there are potholes and there are fewer passing places and we go more slowly. From Ardheslaig the track winds up the hillside to wilder moorland before dropping down to the loch side.

The road continues and turns south and hugs the coast past Callakille and Lonbain. There are distant views across Rona and Raasay to Skye. We can see the Black Cuillins where we climbed the Cuillin Ridge with Jonathan in 1989.

At Applecross we leave the coast and head over the mountains via the

Shieldaig

famous Bealach na Bà or Pass of the Cattle with its amazing switchbacks. This is the most exciting stretch of the whole trip. The narrow Applecross pass road rises gently for the first few miles and then begins to steepen. The land either side of the road is wild and open and excitement begins to build. There is very little other traffic which is just as well. As we approach the pass itself the incline changes and the bends become much tighter and we have to really ride the bike well, leaning into the bend, looking in the direction of travel and counter-steering to get the bike round. It's exhilarating feeling the pressure of the turn through the handlebars of the bike, and the pull of gravity as we lean into the bends. My grip on the bars is relaxed, my arms are bent and my elbows low and it feels like riding a wild horse. This is what it's all about, making it all worthwhile if only for a few moments.

But that was nothing compared to the descent on the other side of the pass. We pulled into the parking at the top of the pass to contemplate the route down, a seeming endless series of hair-pin bends down the steep mountain side. It felt awesome cruising round the shallower bends and taking care of the acute inclines. And it felt satisfying controlling the heavy

Isle of Raasay and Skye from Applecross

bike and getting down safely without incident. The pass continued another five or six miles, easier now, to get back on to the A896 at the Bealach Cafe.

We are back on the two carriageway road and increase speed. The River Kishorn is to our right until we reach civilisation at Loch Carron. At the head of the Loch we turn right on the A890 past Strathcarron. We are tired but it's another 35 miles to the Cluanie Inn in Glen Morrison where we will spend the night. We follow Loch Carron and then crosses over to Loch Alsh where we join the main A87 from Kyle of Lochalsh and the Skye Bridge to Loch Ness. From the causeway that crosses Loch Long at Dornie we get a view of the famous Eilean Donan Castle. From here it's plain sailing along Loch Dulch to Shiel Bridge, The Five Sisters of Kintail are to our left. I came here with the scouts when I was sixteen and climbed all five sisters. The road follows the line of the Old Military Road built in the 18th Century in the wake of the Jacobite Rebellion of 1715 by General George Wade to help suppress any insurrection by the Pretender James Stuart, or his son, Bonnie Prince Charlie.

The Cluanie Inn is situated at the head of Loch Cluanie. The inn dates

Eilean Donan Castle

back to 1787 as a staging post for drovers moving cattle to market in Stirling and Edinburgh. The inn is comfortable and welcoming. The decor emphasises the inn's Scottishness with lots of tartan everywhere. An excellent dinner and a well-earned bed.

Cluanie Inn, Glen

Day 10 Loch Cluanie to Oban 91 miles

Thursday 30 July 2016

It was 90 miles to Oban but we were now on faster roads. The A87 along Loch Garry takes us east in a zigzag to Invergarry and the A82 the main road that follows the Great Glen fault line that cuts across Scotland diagonally from Fort Augustus in the north to Fort William in the south. From there we ride along Loch Lochy to Spean Bridge.

Between Loch Oich and Loch Lochy we run alongside a stretch of the Caledonian Canal. Built in 1810 it links the various lochs in the Great Glen to form a navigation from the east coast of Scotland at Inverness to the west coast at the head of Loch Linnhe. As we passed Torlundy we had great views of Ben Nevis (1344m). We rode through Fort William on the promenade without stopping. Memories of rock and ice climbing on the Ben.

Cluanie Inn

We cross the Ballachulish Bridge and Loch Leven at the end of Glen Coe. When I first started climbing on Ben Nevis you had to drive around the head of the loch at Kinlochleven, a detour of over 20 miles.

Onward along the A829 coast road past Portnacroish, Creagan, the bridge at Dallachulish and the Connel Bridge. Then the A85 into Oban to retrieve the car, reassemble the trailer, load the bike and hitch it to the car and set off for carbo near Edinburgh where we'll spend the night with my sister Lizzie and her husband Alistair. 96 miles to Carbo and then a final 280 miles back home.

It has been a fabulous journey. We drove 688 miles by car and rode 480 miles on the bike. At times, in the rain and cold on Harris it had seemed almost too much for us. But we managed fine, the bike performed brilliantly and, once the sun came out, we had really enjoyed it. But this was the last big trip we made together and we sold the bike and trailer to a young man called Marcus Holland owner of DM Historics, a classic car specialist, who drove all the way from Hadlow in Kent to collect the bike in August 2023. He said he loved old bikes and intended to ride it himself.

No	Date	Day	From	To	Miles	Mode
1	21-Jun-16	Tuesday	Home	Milngavie	257	Car
2	22-Jun-16	Wednesday	Milngavie	Brambles of Inveraray	55	Car
3	23-Jun-16	Thursday	Inveraray	Borve Barra	40	Bike
4	24-Jun-16	Friday	Borve	Nunton House	45	Bike
5	25-Jun-16	Saturday	South Uist	Otter Bunkhouse Lewis	113	Bike
6	26-Jun-16	Sunday	Uig	Cuanna House Stornoway	81	Bike
7	27-Jun-16	Monday	Stornoway	Dundonnel Hotel	26	Bike
8	28-Jun-16	Tuesday	Dundonnel	Cluanie Inn	174	Bike
9	29-Jun-16	Wednesday	Loch Cluanie	Carnbo	96	Car
10	30-Jun-16	Thursday	Edinburgh	Home	280	Car
				TOTAL DRIVE	1167	
				By motorbike	479	
				By car	688	
				By ferry	156	
				TOTAL TRIP	1323	

Plan of the trip

www.ingramcontent.com/pod-product-compliance
Lightning Source LLC
Chambersburg PA
CBHW042341150426
43196CB00001B/19